P9-EDB-065

Goofy Knock-Knocks

Terry Pierce

illustration
Debra Dixon

Sterling Publishing Co., Inc.
New York

To my circle of support:
Mark, Greg, Mailea, Ruth, Cecilia,
and my parents

Library of Congress Cataloging-in-Publication Data

Pierce, Terry.
  Goofy knock-knocks / Terry Pierce ; illustration by Debra Dixon.
    p. cm.
  Includes index.
  ISBN 1-4027-1403-3
  1. Knock-knock jokes. 2. Wit and humor, Juvenile. I. Title.

PN6231.K55P54 2004
818'.602--dc22

                                    2004015546

10 9 8 7 6 5 4 3

Published by Sterling Publishing Co., Inc.
387 Park Avenue South, New York, NY 10016
© 2004 by Terry Pierce
Distributed in Canada by Sterling Publishing
C/o Canadian Manda Group, 165 Dufferin Street
Toronto, Ontario, Canada M6K 3H6
Distributed in the United Kingdom by GMC Distribution Services,
Castle Place, 166 High Street, Lewes, East Sussex, England BN7 1XU
Distributed in Australia by Capricorn Link (Australia) Pty. Ltd.
P.O. Box 704, Windsor, NSW 2756, Australia

Manufactured in the United States of America
All rights reserved

Sterling ISBN-13: 978-1-4027-1403-0 *(hardcover)*
        ISBN-10: 1-4027-1403-3
        ISBN-13: 978-1-4027-2421-3 *(paperback)*
        ISBN-10: 1-4027-2421-7

For information about custom editions, special sales, premium
and corporate purchases, please contact Sterling Special Sales
Department at 800-805-5489 or specialsales@sterlingpub.com.

Knock-knock

Who's there?
Acacia.
  Acacia who?
Acacia forgot, here's my number.

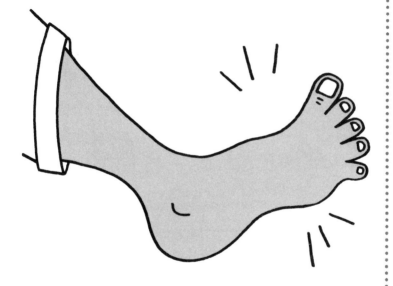

Knock-knock.
  Who's there?
Account.
  Account who?
Account named
Dracula.

Knock-knock.
  Who's there?
Acorn.
  Acorn who?
Acorn is on my foot.

Knock-knock.
Who's there?
Acme.
Acme who?
Acme again later.

Knock-knock.
Who's there?
Al.
Al who?
Al thumbs, aren't you?

Knock-knock.
Who's there?
Adore.
Adore who?
Adore bell is ringing; go answer it!

Knock-knock.
Who's there?
Alaska.
Alaska who?
Alaska next time I see her.

Knock-knock.
Who's there?
Altoona.
Altoona who?
Altoona piano and
sing you a song.

Knock-knock.
Who's there?
Anita.
Anita who?
Anita break from
studying.

Knock-knock.
Who's there?
Ansel.
Ansel who?
Ansel ruin our
picnic.

Knock-knock.
Who's there?
Anson.
Anson who?
Anson my pants
make me do the
boogie dance.

Knock-knock.
Who's there?
Answer.
Answer who?
Answer in our picnic
basket.

Knock-knock.
Who's there?
Arch.
Arch who?
Arch you glad
to see me?

Knock-knock.
  Who's there?
Aroma.
  Aroma who?
Aroma round too much and get lost.

Knock-knock.
  Who's there?
Athena.
  Athena who?
Athena monster under my bed!

Knock-knock.
  Who's there?
Aurora.
  Aurora who?
Aurora is what the lion says.

Knock-knock.
  Who's there?
Avenue.
  Avenue who?
Avenue backpack for school.

Knock-knock

Who's there?
Bacon.
Bacon who?
Bacon a cake?

Knock-knock.
Who's there?
Banana split.
Banana split who?
Banana split—too much fruit in the bowl.

Knock-knock.
Who's there?
Barley.
Barley who?
Barley can hear you. Speak up!

Knock-knock.
Who's there?
Basket.
Basket who?
Basket caught at this
lake all the time.

Knock-knock.
Who's there?
Bass and viol.
Bass and viol who?
Bass it, viol make
mistakes.

Knock-knock.
Who's there?
Bassoon.
Bassoon who?
Bassoon'll be
nibbling at our bait.

Knock-knock.
Who's there?
Bat.
Bat who?
Bat you can't guess
who it is!

Knock-knock.
Who's there?
Batten.
Batten who?
Batten first in the
line-up.

Knock-knock.
Who's there?
Battle.
Battle who?
Battle fly out of the
cave at sunset.

Knock-knock.
Who's there?
Bauble.
Bauble who?
Bauble be home any minute.

Knock-knock.
Who's there?
Begonia.
Begonia who?
Begonia pardon, could you get off my foot!

Knock-knock.
Who's there?
Bison.
Bison who?
Bison-tennial was in 1976.

Knock-knock.
Who's there?
Border.
Border who?
Border to tears with your lecture.

Knock-knock.
Who's there?
Boycott.
Boycott who?
Boycotts are here; girl cots are there.

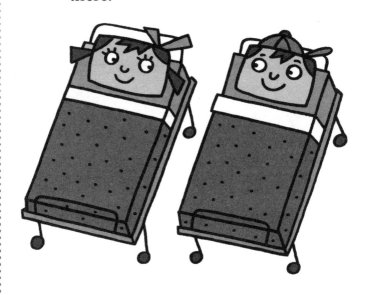

Knock-knock.
Who's there?
Boyds.
Boyds who?
Boyds will be Boyds.

Knock-knock.
  Who's there?
Buckle.
  Buckle who?
Buckle saddle up your horse for you.

Knock-knock.
  Who's there?
Bustle.
  Bustle who?
Bustle be here soon.

Knock-knock.
  Who's there?
Butcher.
  Butcher who?
Butcher right foot in, butcher right foot out...

Knock-knock

Who's there?
Canal.
   Canal who?
Canal come over for dinner?

Knock-knock.
   Who's there?
Canoe.
   Canoe who?
Canoe come to the
phone?

Knock-knock.
   Who's there?
Canopies.
   Canopies who?
Canopies is all we
have for dinner.

Knock-knock.
  Who's there?
Can't chew.
  Can't chew who?
Can't chew open the door?

Knock-knock.
  Who's there?
Cello.
  Cello who?
Cello is my favorite dessert.

Knock-knock.
  Who's there?
Cargo.
  Cargo who?
Cargo beep-beep!

Knock-knock.
  Who's there?
Cement.
  Cement who?
Cement to make you laugh.

Knock-knock.
  Who's there?
CD.
  CD who?
CD doorknob? Turn it so I can come in!

Knock-knock.
  Who's there?
Census.
  Census who?
Census the last day of school, we get a party.

Knock-knock.
Who's there?
Center.
Center who?
Center a birthday card.

Knock-knock.
Who's there?
Cheddar.
Cheddar who?
"Cheddar watch out, Cheddar not cry, Cheddar not pout..."

Knock-knock.
Who's there?
Chooch.
Chooch who?
Here comes the train!

Knock-knock.
Who's there?
Cinch.
Cinch who?
Cinch you're up, open the door!

Knock-knock.
Who's there?
Condemn.
Condemn who?
Condemn kids be on our team?

Knock-knock.
Who's there?
Connecticut.
Connecticut who?
Connecticut the dots.

Knock-knock.
Who's there?
Consult.
Consult who?
Consult make this meal taste any better?

Knock-knock
Who's there?
D. Morey.
  D. Morey who?
D. Morey, de merrier.

Knock-knock.
  Who's there?
Dacey.
  Dacey who?
Dacey better with glasses.

Knock-knock.
  Who's there?
Damali.
  Damali who?
Damali has lots of stores and a movie theatre.

Knock-knock.
Who's there?
Damascus.
Damascus who?
Damascus because it's Halloween.

Knock-knock.
Who's there?
Darby.
Darby who?
Darby a full moon tonight.

Knock-knock.
Who's there?
Darrell.
Darrell who?
Darrell be a spelling test
tomorrow.

Knock-knock.
Who's there?
Decides.
Decides who?
Decides hurt from laughing
at all de knock-knock jokes.

Knock-knock.
Who's there?
Declare.
Declare who?
Declare skies mean good
weather.

Knock-knock.
Who's there?
Decode.
Decode who?
Decode is in my nose.

Knock-knock.
Who's there?
Deduce.
Deduce who?
Deduce is de lowest card in de deck.

Knock-knock.
Who's there?
Design.
Design who?
Design says "Keep off de grass."

Knock-knock.
Who's there?
Despise.
Despise who?
Despise have secret-agent code rings.

Knock-knock.
Who's there?
Detail.
Detail who?
Detail of *Sleeping Beauty* is my favorite.

Knock-knock.
Who's there?
Devote.
Devote who?
Devote goes in de ballot box.

Knock-knock.
Who's there?
Dewayne.
Dewayne who?
Dewayne is getting me wet.

Knock-knock.
Who's there?
Didrika.
Didrika who?
Didrika Ricardo used to live here?

Knock-knock.
Who's there?
Dinosaurs.
Dinosaurs who?
Dinosaurs in hang-gliders.

Knock-knock.
Who's there?
Disguise.
Disguise who?
Disguise bugging me!

Knock-knock.
Who's there?
Dishes.
Dishes who?
Dishes a great joke book.

Knock-knock.
Who's there?
Dolph N.
Dolph N. who?
Dolph N. live in the sea.

Knock-knock.
Who's there?
Donahue.
Donahue who?
Donahue want to let me in?

Knock-knock.
Who's there?
Donatella.
Donatella who?
Donatella me what to do.

Knock-knock.
Who's there?
Dragon.
Dragon who?
Dragon this sled is slowing
me down.

Knock-knock

Who's there?
Earl.
Earl who?
Earl be home for Christmas.

Knock-knock.
Who's there?
Ease.
Ease who?
Ease come after D's.

Knock-knock.
Who's there?
Ease.
Ease who?
Ease at it again.

Knock-knock.
Who's there?
Eclipse.
Eclipse who?
Eclipse hair for a living.

Knock-knock.
Who's there?
Effie and Lactose.
Effie and Lactose who?
Effie you're a snake, then you lactose.

Knock-knock.
Who's there?
Eggs.
Eggs who?
Eggs it out that door.

Knock-knock.
Who's there?
Ego.
Ego who?
Ego fast on his new skates.

Knock-knock.
Who's there?
Eileen Dover.
Eileen Dover who?
Eileen Dover and fell off my bike.

Knock-knock.
Who's there?
Electron.
Electron who?
Electron for class president.

Knock-knock.
Who's there?
Ely.
Ely who?
"Ely Ely O!"

Knock-knock.
Who's there?
Enemy.
Enemy who?
Enemy you'll find a great
friend.

Knock-knock.
Who's there?
Equalize.
Equalize who?
Equalize have 20/20
vision.

Knock-knock.
Who's there?
Era.
Era who?
Era way out of here?

Knock-knock.
Who's there?
Ewe.
Ewe who?
Are you calling me?

Knock-knock.
Who's there?
Excel.
Excel who?
Excel for two dollars
a dozen.

Knock-knock.
Who's there?
Exile.
Exile who?
Exile is next to the
dairy aisle.

Knock-knock

Who's there?
Fangs.
Fangs who?
Fangs a lot!

Knock-knock.
Who's there?
Farrah.
Farrah who?
Farrah skies and
warmer weather.

Knock-knock.
Who's there?
Feud.
Feud who?
Feud practice more
you'd make the
team.

Knock-knock.
Who's there?
Finance.
Finance who?
Finance are married
to fine uncles.

Knock-knock.
Who's there?
Foe.
Foe who?
Foe me? You
shouldn't have!

Knock-knock.
Who's there?
Fleece.
Fleece who?
Fleece Navidad!

Knock-knock.
Who's there?
Folly.
Folly who?
Folly your dreams.

Knock-knock.
Who's there?
Florida.
Florida who?
Florida last time,
stop knocking on my
door!

Knock-knock.
Who's there?
Forest.
Forest who?
Forest the number
after three.

Knock-knock.
Who's there?
Foy.
Foy who?
Foy the last time, let me in!

Knock-knock.
Who's there?
Frasier.
Frasier who?
Frasier going to lose?

Knock-knock.
Who's there?
Freight.
Freight who?
Freight of the dark. Let me in!

Knock-knock.
  Who's there?
Friar.
  Friar who?
Friar up some bacon.

Knock-knock.
  Who's there?
Fuel.
  Fuel who?
Fuel come over here, I'll give you
a hug!

Knock-knock.
  Who's there?
Fulfill.
  Fulfill who?
Fulfill I'd do anything. What
a guy!

Knock-knock

Who's there?
Gadi.
Gadi who?
Gadi minute?

Knock-knock.
Who's there?
Gamma.
Gamma who?
Gamma ball and glove. I'm ready to play ball.

Knock-knock.
Who's there?
Garden.
Garden who?
Garden that cupcake, are you?

Knock-knock.
Who's there?
Gas.
Gas who?
I don't know.
Open the door
so I can see you.

    Knock-knock.
      Who's there?
    Genial.
      Genial who?
    Genial grant you three wishes.

        Knock-knock.
          Who's there?
        Geology.
          Geology who?
        Geology willikers,
        it's good to see you!

Knock-knock.
Who's there?
Gideon.
Gideon who?
Gideon up, horsie!

        Knock-knock.
          Who's there?
        Gigi.
          Gigi who?
        Gigi follows effeff.

Knock-knock.
   Who's there?
Gladys.
   Gladys who?
Gladys Friday.

Knock-knock.
   Who's there?
Goblin.
   Goblin who?
Goblin food gives
you a stomach ache.

Knock-knock.
   Who's there?
Gnu.
   Gnu who?
Gnu shoes?

Knock-knock.
   Who's there?
Gong.
   Gong who?
Gong with the wind.

Knock-knock.
   Who's there?
Gobi.
   Gobi who?
Gobi a ghost for
Halloween.

Knock-knock.
   Who's there?
Gopher.
   Gopher who?
Gopher it!

Knock-knock.
Who's there?
Gown.
Gown who?
Gown fishing.

Knock-knock.
Who's there?
Graceland.
Graceland who?
Graceland the plane
well, didn't she?

Knock-knock.
Who's there?
Grammar.
Grammar who?
Grammar and
Grandpa. Let us in!

Knock-knock.
Who's there?
Gus.
Gus who?
Gus who it is, silly!

Knock-knock

Who's there?
Habib.
Habib who?
Habib is worn by a baby.

Knock-knock.
Who's there?
Habit.
Habit who?
Habit loaning me a dollar?

Knock-knock.
Who's there?
Hair.
Hair who?
Hair I am again.

Knock-knock.
  Who's there?
Hali and Bea.
  Hali and Bea who?
Hali-ween is coming,
so Bea-ware of
ghosts!

Knock-knock.
  Who's there?
Hamal.
  Hamal who?
Hamal choked up.

Knock-knock.
  Who's there?
Hannah.
  Hannah who?
Hannah one,
Hannah two...

Knock-knock.
  Who's there?
Harry S Truman.
  *Harry S Truman
who?*
Harry S Truman of
his word.

Knock-knock.
  Who's there?
Harvey.
  Harvey who?
Harvey there yet?

Knock-knock.
  Who's there?
Hawaii.
  Hawaii who?
Hawaii you doing?

Knock-knock.
Who's there?
Hello bull.
Hello bull who?
Are you having a party?

Knock-knock.
Who's there?
Hera.
Hera who?
"Hera we go 'round the mulberry bush..."

Knock-knock.
Who's there?
Hero.
Hero who?
Hero the boat to shore.

Knock-knock.
   Who's there?
Hertz.
   Hertz who?
Hertz when you say
mean things to me!

Knock-knock.
   Who's there?
Hobbit.
   Hobbit who?
Hobbit off more than
I can chew.

Knock-knock.
   Who's there?
Hewlett.
   Hewlett who?
Hewlett the dog out?

Knock-knock.
   Who's there?
Honeydew.
   Honeydew who?
Honeydew me a
favor and open the
door.

Knock-knock.
   Who's there?
Hiram.
   Hiram who?
Hiram to deliver
newspapers.

Knock-knock.
   Who's there?
Howard.
   Howard who?
Howard you like
them apples?

Knock-knock.
Who's there?
Howell.
Howell who?
Howell I come in if you don't open the door?

Knock-knock.
Who's there?
Howl.
Howl who?
Howl I ever repay you?

Knock-knock.
Who's there?
Hugh.
Hugh who?
Hugh da man!

Knock-knock

Who's there?
Ice cream.
Ice cream who?
Ice cream on the roller coaster.

Knock-knock.
Who's there?
Ice water.
Ice water who?
Ice water flies.

Knock-knock.
Who's there?
Icicle.
Icicle who?
Icicle little bit after eating too much cake.

Knock-knock.
Who's there?
Icing.
Icing who?
Icing in a band.

Knock-knock.
Who's there?
Icon.
Icon who?
Icon do anything I set my
mind to.

Knock-knock.
Who's there?
Icy snow.
Icy snow who?
Icy snow on the mountains.

Knock-knock.
Who's there?
Indy.
Indy who?
Indy long run,
you'll be sorry.

Knock-knock.
Who's there?
India.
India who?
India refrigerator you'll find
cold food.

Knock-knock.
Who's there?
Into.
Into who?
Into minutes, it'll be halftime.

Knock-knock.
Who's there?
Iona.
Iona who?
Iona bike.

Knock-knock.
Who's there?
Iowa.
Iowa who?
Iowa you a lot.

Knock-knock.
Who's there?
Isaac.
Isaac who?
Isaac with the flu.

Knock-knock.
Who's there?
Isabella.
Isabella who?
Isabella working? I had to knock.

Knock-knock.
Who's there?
Isaiah.
Isaiah who?
Isaiah it again, "Knock-knock."

Knock-knock.
Who's there?
Ishmael.
Ishmael who?
Ishmael in the mailbox?

Knock-knock.
Who's there?
Issue.
Issue coming over to play?

    Knock-knock.
      Who's there?
    Itch.
      Itch who?
    Gesundheit!

        Knock-knock.
          Who's there?
        Italia.
          Italia who?
        Italia, things could be worse.

Knock-knock.
  Who's there?
Ivana.
  Ivana who?
Ivana play.

Knock-knock

Who's there?
Jackal.
Jackal who?
Jackal get caught by the giant.

Knock-knock.
Who's there?
Jackson.
Jackson who?
Jackson marbles are my favorite games.

Knock-knock.
Who's there?
Jamaica.
Jamaica who?
Jamaica me wait here too long!

Knock-knock.
Who's there?
Javier.
Javier who?
Javier been to a
play?

Knock-knock.
Who's there?
Jeer.
Jeer who?
Jeer about the big
test?

Knock-knock.
Who's there?
Jenelle.
Jenelle who?
Jenelle the door shut?

Knock-knock.
Who's there?
Jerky.
Jerky who?
Jerky working? Then
unlock the door.

Knock-knock.
Who's there?
Jess.
Jess who?
Jess let me in.

Knock-knock.
Who's there?
Jewel.
Jewel who?
Jewel be our goalie.

Knock-knock.
Who's there?
José.
José who?
"José can you see, by
the dawn's early
light..."

Knock-knock.
Who's there?
Joust.
Joust who?
Joust me.

Knock-knock.
Who's there?
Juana.
Juana who?
Juana see a movie?

Knock-knock.
Who's there?
Juicy.
Juicy who?
Juicy the size of that bug?

Knock-knock.
Who's there?
July.
July who?
July again? You need
to start telling the truth.

Knock-knock.
Who's there?
Jupiter.
Jupiter who?
Jupiter rock in my shoe?

Knock-knock.
Who's there?
Just Ashen.
Just Ashen who?
Just Ashen for directions.

Knock-knock.
Who's there?
Justice.
Justice who?
Justice chickens!

Knock-knock.
Who's there?
Justin.
Justin who?
Justin case you want to call,
here's my number.

Knock-knock

Who's there?
Kai.
  Kai who?
Kai come in?

Knock-knock.
  Who's there?
Kanga.
  Kanga who?
What are you? Part kangaroo and part owl?

Knock-knock.
  Who's there?
Kansas.
  Kansas who?
Kansas be true?

Knock-knock.
Who's there?
Kara.
Kara who?
Kara let me in?

Knock-knock.
Who's there?
Katie.
Katie who?
Katie letter that comes after J.

Knock-knock.
Who's there?
Kareem.
Kareem who?
Kareem of the crop.

Knock-knock.
Who's there?
Keanu.
Keanu who?
Keanu key chain.

Knock-knock.
Who's there?
Karsen.
Karsen who?
Karsen the shop getting fixed.

Knock-knock.
Who's there?
Kelda.
Kelda who?
Kelda mosquito on my leg.

Knock-knock.
  Who's there?
Kenda.
  Kenda who?
Kenda car go any
faster?

Knock-knock.
  Who's there?
Kerri.
  Kerri who?
Kerri my books?

Knock-knock.
  Who's there?
Kennedy.
  Kennedy who?
Kennedy window be
opened?

Knock-knock.
  Who's there?
Kiki.
  Kiki who?
Kiki the ball past the
goalie.

Knock-knock.
Who's there?
Kipper.
Kipper who?
Kipper hands to
yourself.

Knock-knock.
Who's there?
Klaus.
Klaus who?
Klaus your books
and get ready for the
test.

Knock-knock.
Who's there?
Koala T.
Koala T. who?
Koala T. is more
important than
quantity.

Knock-knock.
Who's there?
Kook.
Kook who?
Kook-who clock.

Knock-knock.
Who's there?
Kristof.
Kristof who?
Kristof all the things
on my list.

Knock-knock.
Who's there?
Kurt C.
Kurt C. who?
Kurt C. if you're a
girl, bow if you're a
boy.

L

Knock-knock

Who's there?
Lattice.
Lattice who?
Lattice hold hands and sing.

Knock-knock.
Who's there?
Lazy.
Lazy who?
Lazy blanket on ze cot.

Knock-knock.
Who's there?
Lecture.
Lecture who?
Lecture hair down and have some fun.

Knock-knock.
Who's there?
Leena.
Leena who?
Leena little closer
and I'll tell you a
secret.

Knock-knock.
Who's there?
Les.
Les who?
Les get this show on
the road!

Knock-knock.
Who's there?
Lesson.
Lesson who?
Lesson five minutes
and school's out for
summer!

Knock-knock.
Who's there?
Lichen.
Lichen who?
Lichen my jokes,
aren't you?

Knock-knock.
Who's there?
Lilian Bill.
Lilian Bill who?
Lilian Bill are
coming to my party.

Knock-knock.
Who's there?
Linus.
Linus who?
Linus over there for
ticket holders.

Knock-knock.
Who's there?
Lion.
Lion who?
Lion down on the job
again?

Knock-knock.
Who's there?
Liotta.
Liotta who?
Liotta study for the test.

Knock-knock.
Who's there?
Lois.
Lois who?
Lois man on the totem pole.

Knock-knock.
Who's there?
Luke.
Luke who?
Luke out below!

Knock-knock.
Who's there?
Lunge.
Lunge who?
Lunge is served in the cafeteria.

Knock-knock

Who's there?
Macon.
Macon who?
Macon the most of it.

M

Knock-knock.
Who's there?
Madge.
Madge who?
Madge you look!

Knock-knock.
Who's there?
Maia.
Maia who?
Maia, oh, my; its
good to see you.

Knock-knock.
Who's there?
Maine.
Maine who?
Maine thing is, take care of yourself.

Knock-knock.
Who's there?
Mako shark.
Mako shark who?
Mako shark leave me alone.

Knock-knock.
Who's there?
Marge.
Marge who?
Marge two, three, four; to the rear, two, three, four!

Knock-knock.
Who's there?
Marietta.
Marietta who?
Marietta good breakfast before school.

Knock-knock.
Who's there?
Mauro.
Mauro who?
Mauro that good Thanksgiving turkey, please!

Knock-knock.
Who's there?
Maximilian.
Maximilian who?
Maximilian laughs a minute.

Knock-knock.
Who's there?
Melody.
Melody who?
Melody cards before the holiday rush.

Knock-knock.
Who's there?
Meringue.
Meringue who?
Meringue the
doorbell twice.

Knock-knock.
Who's there?
Michelle.
Michelle who?
Michelle phone is
broken. Can I borrow
yours?

Knock-knock.
Who's there?
Midori.
Midori who?
Midori is always
open for you.

Knock-knock.
Who's there?
Mikasa.
Mikasa who?
Mikasa es su casa.

Knock-knock.
Who's there?
Mike Guntry.
Mike Guntry who?
"Mike Guntry tis of thee,
sweet land of liberty..."

Knock-knock.
Who's there?
Millard Fillmore.
Millard Fillmore who?
Millard Fillmore buckets
than you.

Knock-knock.
Who's there?
Millicent.
Millicent who?
Millicent me a postcard.

Knock-knock.
Who's there?
Milo S.
Milo S. who?
Milo S. grade was a B.

Knock-knock.
Who's there?
Minnesota.
Minnesota who?
Minnesota is
a tiny drink.

Knock-knock.
Who's there?
Miso.
Miso who?
Miso hungry. Can I stay for dinner?

Knock-knock.
Who's there?
Mistake.
Mistake who?
Mistake is done. Let's eat!

Knock-knock.
Who's there?
Mississippi.
Mississippi who?
Mississippi. I'm Mr. Ippi's wife.

Knock-knock.
Who's there?
Mixture.
Mixture who?
Mixture Rogers.

Knock-knock.
Who's there?
Missouri.
Missouri who?
Missouri loves company.

Knock-knock.
Who's there?
Myth.
Myth who?
Myth me while I wath away?

Knock-knock

Who's there?
N. Kaycee.
N. Kaycee who?
N. Kaycee you need me, just call.

Knock-knock.
Who's there?
Nacho.
Nacho who?
It's nacho best friend.

Knock-knock.
Who's there?
Nadia.
Nadia who?
Nadia your head if you agree with me.

Knock-knock.
Who's there?
Nanette.
Nanette who?
Nanette the last
biscuit.

Knock-knock.
Who's there?
Napkin.
Napkin who?
Napkin in class
again?

Knock-knock.
Who's there?
Needle.
Needle who?
Needle help getting
in?

Knock-knock.
Who's there?
Nettle.
Nettle who?
Nettle be used for
catching butterflies.

Knock-knock.
Who's there?
New Jersey.
New Jersey who?
New Jersey you're
wearing?

Knock-knock.
Who's there?
Noah.
Noah who?
Noah good book to
read?

Knock-knock.
Who's there?
Normal.
Normal who?
Normal be back in a
few minutes.

Knock-knock

Who's there?
O. Wanda.
  O. Wanda who?
"O. Wanda saints, come marching in..."

Knock-knock.
  Who's there?
Obey.
  Obey who?
Obey-wan Kenobi.

Knock-knock.
  Who's there?
Odd.
  Odd who?
Odd open the door, if
I were you.

Knock-knock.
Who's there?
Odessa.
Odessa who?
Odessa really nice
bike!

Knock-knock.
Who's there?
Odor.
Odor who?
Odor the hill.

Knock-knock.
Who's there?
Omelet.
Omelet who?
Omelet you in so
you'll stop ringing
the bell.

Knock-knock.
Who's there?
Ooze.
Ooze who?
Ooze the boss?

Knock-knock.
Who's there?
Oprah.
Oprah who?
Oprah singer.

Knock-knock.
Who's there?
Oral.
Oral who?
Oral huff and I'll
puff and I'll blow
your house down!

Knock-knock.
Who's there?
Orbit.
Orbit who?
Orbit my tongue.

61

Knock-knock.
Who's there?
Orchid.
Orchid who?
Orchid around a lot
with knock-knock
jokes.

Knock-knock.
Who's there?
Orma.
Orma who?
Orma really nice
guy.

Knock-knock.
Who's there?
Ornament.
Ornament who?
Ornament it, I'll be
ready.

Knock-knock.
Who's there?
Osborn.
Osborn who?
Osborn in Texas.

Knock-knock.
Who's there?
Ostrich.
Ostrich who?
Ostrich the rubber
band until it
snapped.

Knock-knock.
Who's there?
Otter.
Otter who?
Otter let me in.

Knock-knock.
Who's there?
Outstanding.
Outstanding who?
Outstanding in the
rain again. Open up!

Knock-knock

Who's there?
Panel.
Panel who?
Panel get hot if you leave it on the fire.

Knock-knock.
Who's there?
Paolo.
Paolo who?
Paolo 'round with me?

Knock-knock.
Who's there?
Papa.
Papa who?
Papa goes the weasel!

Knock-knock.
  Who's there?
Parish.
  Parish who?
Parish shoes.

Knock-knock.
  Who's there?
Passion.
  Passion who?
Passion notes in class
will get you in trouble.

Knock-knock.
  Who's there?
Pasta.
  Pasta who?
Pasta salt, please.

Knock-knock.
Who's there?
Peace.
Peace who?
Peace and carrots.

Knock-knock.
Who's there?
Piccolo.
Piccolo who?
Piccolo number.

Knock-knock.
Who's there?
Pheasant.
Pheasant who?
Pheasant this a nice
surprise!

Knock-knock.
Who's there?
Picnic.
Picnic who?
Picnic. He's a good
pitcher.

Knock-knock.
Who's there?
Phoebe.
Phoebe who?
Phoebe expensive for
an overdue library
book.

Knock-knock.
Who's there?
Pika.
Pika who?
Pika card, any card.

Knock-knock.
Who's there?
Ping.
Ping who?
Ping-pong anyone?

    Knock-knock.
      Who's there?
    Planet.
      Planet who?
    Planet well.

    Knock-knock.
      Who's there?
    Police.
      Police who?
    Police don't slam
    the door.

Knock-knock.
Who's there?
Porter.
Porter who?
Porter milk on
my cereal.

    Knock-knock.
      Who's there?
    Pressure.
      Pressure who?
    Pressure face against
    the glass.

66

Knock-knock.
Who's there?
Presta.
Presta who?
Presta seam on my pants.

Knock-knock.
Who's there?
Promise.
Promise who?
Promise for high school students.

Knock-knock.
Who's there?
Purchase.
Purchase who?
Purchase for birds to sit on.

Knock-knock.
Who's there?
Pudding.
Pudding who?
Pudding all your eggs in one basket?

Knock-knock

Who's there?
Quack.
Quack who?
Quack in the sidewalk.

Knock-knock.
Who's there?
Quark.
Quark who?
Quark Kent.

Knock-knock.
Who's there?
Quarter.
Quarter who?
Quarter milk and a box of cereal for the family breakfast.

Knock-knock.
Who's there?
Quartz.
Quartz who?
Quartz are for
playing basketball
and tennis.

Knock-knock.
Who's there?
Queen.
Queen who?
Queen up the
cwassroom before the
teacher comes back.

Knock-knock.
Who's there?
Quench.
Quench who?
Quench the handle
before you swing the
bat.

Knock-knock.
Who's there?
Quick.
Quick who?
Quick your heels
three times and
make a wish.

Knock-knock.
Who's there?
Quiet.
Quiet who?
Quiet a place you've
got here.

Knock-knock.
Who's there?
Quill.
Quill who?
Quill you just open
the door!

Knock-knock.
   Who's there?
Quilt.
   Quilt who?
Quilt while you're ahead.

Knock-knock.
   Who's there?
Quip.
   Quip who?
Quip my hair, please.

Knock-knock.
   Who's there?
Quiver.
   Quiver who?
Quiver a break!

Knock-knock
Who's there?
Ransom.
Ransom who?
Ransom of the way, walked the rest.

Knock-knock.
Who's there?
Raptor.
Raptor who?
Raptor up for the Halloween party.

Knock-knock.
Who's there?
Rapture.
Rapture who?
Rapture presents all by myself.

Knock-knock.
   Who's there?
Ratio.
   Ratio who?
Ratio to the end of
the street.

Knock-knock.
   Who's there?
Rin.
   Rin who?
Rin here as fast as I
could.

Knock-knock.
   Who's there?
Raven.
   Raven who?
Raven about your
new skateboard
again?

Knock-knock.
   Who's there?
Ringo.
   Ringo who?
Ringo 'round the rosy.

Knock-knock.
   Who's there?
Rhoda.
   Rhoda who?
Rhoda boat with
these oars

Knock-knock.
   Who's there?
Rita.
   Rita who?
Rita good book.

Knock-knock.
Who's there?
Rook.
Rook who?
Rook out below!

Knock-knock.
Who's there?
Rowdy.
Rowdy who?
Rowdy boat faster.

Knock-knock.
Who's there?
Rowena.
Rowena who?
Rowena the boat as fast as I can!

Knock-knock.
Who's there?
Rubber.
Rubber who?
Rubber the wrong way and you're in trouble.

Knock-knock

Who's there?
Safari.
Safari who?
Safari so good.

Knock-knock.
Who's there?
Sahara.
Sahara who?
Sahara on your head is standing straight up.

Knock-knock.
Who's there?
Sancho.
Sancho who?
Sancho a birthday card. Did you get it?

74

Knock-knock.
Who's there?
Sandy.
Sandy who?
Sandy Claus.

Knock-knock.
Who's there?
Shamus.
Shamus who?
Shamus going to
rain on our picnic.

Knock-knock.
Who's there?
Sherlock.
Sherlock who?
Sherlock is broken so
I walked on in.

Knock-knock.
Who's there?
Sioux Falls.
Sioux Falls who?
Sioux Falls a lot.
She's kind of clumsy.

Knock-knock.
Who's there?
Soda.
Soda who?
Soda you want to see
a movie?

Knock-knock.
Who's there?
Sonia.
Sonia who?
Sonia own clothes?

Knock-knock.
Who's there?
Stefan.
Stefan who?
Stefan the gas; we're
late!

Knock-knock.
Who's there?
Sven.
Sven who?
Sven comes after svix.

Knock-knock.
Who's there?
Summer.
Summer who?
Summer better than others.

Knock-knock.
Who's there?
Suzuki.
Suzuki who?
Suzuki's in the zookeeper's pocket.

Knock-knock.
Who's there?
Synonym.
Synonym who?
Synonym rolls, anyone?

Knock-knock

Who's there?
Taco.
Taco who?
Taco little louder, I can't hear you!

Knock-knock.
Who's there?
Talon.
Talon who?
Talon on people isn't nice.

Knock-knock.
Who's there?
Tank.
Tank who?
Tank goodness you finally let me in!

Knock-knock.
Who's there?
Tennis shoe.
Tennis shoe who?
Tennis shoe lucky
number.

Knock-knock.
Who's there?
Tern.
Tern who?
Tern the doorknob so
I can come in.

Knock-knock.
Who's there?
Texas.
Texas who?
Texas a mighty big guy.

Knock-knock.
Who's there?
Thane.
Thane who?
Thane joke, different
day.

Knock-knock.
Who's there?
Thatcher.
Thatcher who?
Thatcher new bike?

Knock-knock.
Who's there?
Theo.
Theo who?
Theo later, alligator.

Knock-knock.
Who's there?
Thermos.
Thermos who?
Thermos be an easier
way to do this.

Knock-knock.
  Who's there?
Thomas.
  Thomas who?
Thomas of the
essence.

Knock-knock.
  Who's there?
Toodle.
  Toodle who?
Are you leaving? I
just got here!

Knock-knock.
  Who's there?
Tim.
  Tim who?
Tim-ber!

Knock-knock.
  Who's there?
Toot.
  Toot who?
That's what a
ballerina wears.

Knock-knock.
  Who's there?
Torres.
  Torres who?
Torres pants when he bent over.

  Knock-knock.
    Who's there?
  Tree ducks.
    Tree ducks who?
  Tree ducks laid tree eggs.

    Knock-knock.
      Who's there?
    Tuba.
      Tuba who?
    Tuba toothpaste.

Knock-knock.
  Who's there?
Tucker.
  Tucker who?
Tucker in bed and read her a story.

Knock-knock

Who's there?
Udder.
Udder who?
"Udder the river and through the woods, to Grandmother's house we go..."

Knock-knock.
Who's there?
Ugo.
Ugo who?
Ugo first.

Knock-knock.
Who's there?
Ulani.
Ulani who?
Ulani needs to be watered.

Knock-knock.
Who's there?
Ulysses Grant.
Ulysses Grant who?
Ulysses Grants his
wish.

Knock-knock.
Who's there?
Undo.
Undo who?
Undo wear.

Knock-knock.
Who's there?
Unit.
Unit who?
Unit me a sweater?

Knock-knock.
Who's there?
Upton.
Upton who?
Upton now, I
couldn't dance.

Knock-knock.
Who's there?
Urania.
Urania who?
Urania on my
parade.

Knock-knock.
Who's there?
Urge.
Urge who?
Urge you listening.

Knock-knock.
Who's there?
Uri.
Uri who?
Uri nice guy.

Knock-knock.
Who's there?
Utah.
Utah who?
Utah's the ball to
me.

Knock-knock

Who's there?
Vance.
Vance who?
Vance in a blue moon.

Knock-knock.
Who's there?
Vanessa.
Vanessa who?
Vanessa all gassed
up and ready to go.

Knock-knock.
Who's there?
Vasha.
Vasha who?
Vasha your hands
before eating.

Knock-knock.
Who's there?
Venda.
Venda who?
Venda bell rings,
open da door.

Knock-knock.
Who's there?
Vent.
Vent who?
Vent for a valk and
vanted to visit.

Knock-knock.
Who's there?
Verrill B.
Verrill B. who?
Verrill B. a big party
on the last day of
school.

Knock-knock.
Who's there?
Viper.
Viper who?
Viper windshield
clean.

Knock-knock.
Who's there?
Vonda.
Vonda who?
Vonda count of
three, smile!

Knock-knock

Who's there?
Waa.
Waa who?
What are you so happy about?

Knock-knock.
Who's there?
Wade.
Wade who?
Wade a while and I'll knock again.

Knock-knock.
Who's there?
Waddle.
Waddle who?
Waddle you give me to stop telling knock-knock jokes?

Knock-knock.
    Who's there?
Wafer.
    Wafer who?
Wafer your turn.

Knock-knock.
    Who's there?
Waldo.
    Waldo who?
Waldo wall carpet.

Knock-knock.
    Who's there?
Wanda.
    Wanda who?
Wanda hear another joke?

Knock-knock.
    Who's there?
Waseem.
    Waseem who?
Waseem like a hard test turned out to be easy.

Knock-knock.
    Who's there?
Wes.
    Wes who?
Wes new with you?

Knock-knock.
    Who's there?
Weston.
    Weston who?
Weston peace.

Knock-knock.
    Who's there?
Wet.
    Wet who?
Wet me in. I'm fweezing!

Knock-knock.
Who's there?
Whale watch.
Whale watch who?
Whale watch you waiting for?
Open the door!

Knock-knock.
Who's there?
Wheaton.
Wheaton who?
Wheaton for you
to open the door.

Knock-knock.
Who's there?
Whittle.
Whittle who?
Whittle it be, ma'am?

Knock-knock.
Who's there?
Who.
Who who?
Nice owl impression.

Knock-knock.
Who's there?
Wildebeest.
Wildebeest who?
Wildebeest and de Beauty
live happily ever after?

Knock-knock.
   Who's there?
Windy.
   Windy who?
Windy bell rings, it's
time for recess.

Knock-knock.
   Who's there?
Winslow.
   Winslow who?
Winslow, lose fast.

Knock-knock.
   Who's there?
Wise.
   Wise who?
Wise your door
always locked?

Knock-knock.
   Who's there?
Woo.
   Woo who?
Woo-hoo! It's
summer vacation!

Knock-knock.
   Who's there?
Woodchuck.
   Woodchuck who?
Woodchuck like to be
on our team?

Knock-knock.
   Who's there?
Wooden.
   Wooden who?
Wooden you like to
see me?

Knock-knock.
   Who's there?
Wren.
   Wren who?
Wren all the way to
school.

Knock-knock.
  Who's there?
Wyatt D. Elephant.
  Wyatt D. Elephant who?
Wyatt D. Elephant cross the lions?
To get to the other pride.

Knock-knock.
  Who's there?
Wyndham.
  Wyndham who?
Wyndham cookies are done,
let's eat them!

Knock-knock

Who's there?
Xander.
Xander who?
Xander over to my house to play.

Knock-knock.
Who's there?
Xanthus.
Xanthus who?
Xanthus at the
beach.

Knock-knock.
Who's there?
Xenia.
Xenia who?
Xenia hanging out at
the mall.

Knock-knock.
Who's there?
Xaria.
Xaria who?
Xaria doctor in the
house?

Knock-knock.
Who's there?
Xerox.
Xerox who?
Xerox on this farm?

Knock-knock.
Who's there?
Xavier.
Xavier who?
Xavier yourself!
Abandon ship!

Knock-knock.
Who's there?
Xylophone.
Xylophone who?
Xylophone home.

Knock-knock

Who's there?
Ya.
Ya who?
Pretty excited to see me, aren't you?

Knock-knock.
Who's there?
Yancy.
Yancy who?
Yancy nothing yet.

Knock-knock.
Who's there?
Yankee.
Yankee who?
Yankee chain to ring
the bell.

Knock-knock.
Who's there?
Yap-yap-yap.
Yap-yap-yap who?
"Yap-yap-yap,"
said the coyote
in the desert.

Knock-knock.
Who's there?
Yarrow.
Yarrow who?
Yarrow me a quarter.

Knock-knock.
Who's there?
Yawl.
Yawl who?
Yawl come back now,
y' hear?

Knock-knock.
Who's there?
Yearbook.
Yearbook who?
Yearbook is overdue.

Knock-knock.
Who's there?
Yoke.
Yoke who?
Yoke's on you!

Knock-knock.
Who's there?
Yule log.
Yule log who?
Yule log onto the
computer first.

Knock-knock.
Who's there?
Yolanda.
Yolanda who?
Yolanda big fish!

Knock-knock.
  Who's there?
You.
  You who?
Are you calling me?

Knock-knock.
  Who's there?
Yucatan.
  Yucatan who?
Yucatan catch more
flies with honey than
vinegar.

Knock-knock.
  Who's there?
Yule.
  Yule who?
Yule be glad when I
run out of knock-
knock jokes.

Knock-knock.
  Who's there?
Yuma.
  Yuma who?
Yuma best friend.

Z

Knock-knock

Who's there?
Zamora.
Zamora who?
Zamora cake and ice cream, please.

Knock-knock.
Who's there?
Zaza.
Zaza who?
Zaza lot of knock-knock jokes.

Knock-knock.
Who's there?
Zeal.
Zeal who?
Zeal it with a kiss.

94

Knock-knock.
Who's there?
Zelda.
Zelda who?
Zelda skates since they don't fit you anymore.

Knock-knock.
Who's there?
Zenda.
Zenda who?
Zenda large pepperoni pizza and make it quick!

Knock-knock.
Who's there?
Zephyr.
Zephyr who?
Zephyr is on ze cat.

Knock-knock.
Who's there?
Zinc.
Zinc who?
Zinc I was really out of knock-knock jokes?

Knock-knock.
Who's there?
Zinc oxide.
Zinc oxide who?
Zinc oxide the box.

Knock-knock.
Who's there?
Zombies.
Zombies who?
Zombies make honey.

Knock-knock.
Who's there?
Zounds.
Zounds who?
Zounds like the last knock-knock joke!

Index